Tam and the Hat

By Sally Cowan

Tam has a hat.

Reb sits.

Rib the rat sits in her cap.

I can hit the hat.

Tip, tip, tap!

I bet Pip is in my hat.

Sit, Pip! Sit, Reb!

I can hit my hat.

Tip, tip, tap!

I bet Rib is in the hat!

Reb, is Rib in the hat?

I can tip the hat.

Rib **is** in my hat!

CHECKING FOR MEANING

1. Where is Rib sitting at the start of the story? *(Literal)*

2. What sound does Tam make when she hits the hat? *(Literal)*

3. Why do you think Tam keeps finding different animals in the hat? *(Inferential)*

EXTENDING VOCABULARY

hat	Look at the word *hat*. Which sounds are in this word? Which sound is changed to turn *hat* into *hit*?
tip	Look at the illustrations and think about what the word *tip* means in the story. What does Tam do when she tips the hat?
Pip	Which words can you use to describe *Pip*, the rabbit? What does Pip look like? How does Pip feel to touch? What sounds might Pip make?

MOVING BEYOND THE TEXT

1. How do you think Tam feels when Rib and Pip are in her hat? Why?

2. What other animals could Tam put in her hat? Why?

3. Do you think Tam can really do magic?

4. What other tricks do magicians often do?

SPEED SOUNDS

| Cc | Bb | Rr | Ee | Ff | Hh | Nn |

| Mm | Ss | Aa | Pp | Ii | Tt |

PRACTICE WORDS

Reb

hat

Rib

in

rat

cap

hit

can

bet